D0118956

Beautiful
Seattle

Beautiful
Seattle

Concept and Design: Robert D. Shangle
Text: Ann Rule

First Printing October, 1979
Published by Beautiful America Publishing Company
P.O. Box 608, Beaverton, Oregon 97075
Robert D. Shangle, Publisher

Library of Congress Cataloging in Publication Data
Beautiful Seattle
1. Seattle—Description—Views. I. Rule, Ann
F899.S443B4   979.7'77   79-23392
ISBN 0-89802-071-9
ISBN 0-89802-070-0 (paperback)

Photo Credits

ED COOPER—*pages 36-37; page 49.*

JOHN GRONERT—*page 33.*

JOHN HILL—*page 17; page 24; page 52-53; page 56.*

HUGH McKENNA—*page 57; page 60.*

ROY MONTGOMERY—*page 40.*

PAT O'HARA—*page 28.*

CECIL RILEY—*pages 20-21.*

STEVE TERRILL—*page 18; page 19; page 22; page 23; page 25; page 27; page 29; page 30; page 31; page 32; page 34; page 35; page 38; page 39; page 41; page 42; page 43; page 44; page 45; page 46; page 47; page 48; page 50; page 51; page 54; page 55; page 58; page 59; page 61; page 62; page 63; page 64.*

Enlarged Prints

Most of the photography in this book is available as photographic enlargements. Send self-addressed, stamped envelope for information.
For a complete product catalog, send $1.00.
Beautiful America Publishing Company
P.O. Box 608
Beaverton, Oregon 97075

Lithographed in the U.S.A. by Fremont Litho, Fremont, California

Contents

Introduction

Seattle, in many ways, was the last frontier of major American cities. Located in the furthermost northwest corner of the United States, there was nothing beyond to the west but the Pacific Ocean, and, to the north, the Canadian border. To the pioneers of the 1800s who struggled across the awesome and treacherous summits of the Cascade Mountains, the land that was to become Seattle was a miracle, stretching out before them just as they believed that all was lost.

Seattle is still a young city, a place where anything is possible. Friendly, welcoming, and dynamic, Seattle's air is fresh and clean, its scenery is spectacular, and the living is easy. Despite the fact that folks east of the Mississippi tend to believe that cowboys and Indians might still abound in the Queen City, and fiction writers seeking to banish characters forever send them to Seattle, the city is alive, well, and booming. There is no better place to live.

Seattle is a city dominated by water, some 25 miles of land stretching north and south, bordered on either side by vast bodies of water, and laced with waterways and lakes in the very midst of the city. Even on downtown streets, one may pause to enjoy the clear blue vista of Puget Sound and the seagulls gliding effortlessly over the ferry boats, to breathe in the tang of sea air.

The Olympic Mountain range and the snow-crested magnificence of Mount Rainier seem almost within arm's length to those traveling the freeways in downtown Seattle, so compelling in their beauty that even long-time residents catch their breath at the sight.

Yesterday and today exist side-by-side in Seattle. Soaring skyscrapers that seem to be built entirely of glass are but a few steps from carefully preserved buildings of aged brick decorated with ornate gargoyles. Pioneer and Occidental Squares retain their brick paving, pergolas, and gas lights. Indeed, the old Seattle remains today underground, covered over after the holocaust that leveled the city in the Great Fire of 1889. It is a dank and eerie remembrance of a time long past—and a fascinating lure for tourists. The ashes of the lost-forever buildings of that first Seattle were barely cool before the rebuilding began. Streets were raised from eight to 35 feet, leaving structures below as they had been.

When taking the Underground Tour, one almost expects to see a citizen or two from the Seattle of the 1880s appear along those deserted and dank streets where the sun never filters in. The tour operates six days a week, beginning at Doc Maynard's Restaurant—an eatery named for one of Seattle's most colorful founders, a man known both for his vision and his vast capacity for the grape.

Because Nature herself has blessed Seattle with the most breathtaking site possible, city planners as well as every-day citizens have fought to preserve and build pockets of serenity and beauty throughout the city. Parks abound everywhere—some no bigger than a tiny lot, some many acres in size. If a flower, bush, or tree will grow, the soil is planted and cultivated, and everyone can enjoy a break from the demands of the city.

Seattleites realize that the city's prodigious rainfall is largely responsible for the lushness of its vegetation, and, rather than cursing the rain, they welcome it. Although, as the song proclaims optimistically, "The bluest skies you'll ever see are in Seattle . . . ," and there *are* many days when the sky above is a clear azure blue, there are many more when the rain pelts down in silver sheets. It is so common that few long-time residents bother with umbrellas; the rain is just *there*, and Seattleites thrive on it. A growing underground group, which calls itself "Lesser Seattle" and wants to keep the population at its present half-million, distributes bumper stickers reading, "Seattle Rain Festival—September to June," in the frail hope that newcomers will be discouraged! The campaign is more in fun than in unfriendliness; those who do move to Seattle are quickly accepted into the mainstream.

One of the principal draws to Seattle is the fact that it is situated geographically so that, within a span of two hours, one can be in an entirely different world . . . on the summit of a snow-capped mountain where the skiing is superb; on a Pacific Ocean beach, walking along a forest trail where 200-year-old fir trees tower overhead; sailing to an island in the San Juans; or driving through the rolling hills of Eastern Washington, covered as far as the eye can see with shimmering wheat. There are old mining towns of Black Diamond and Wilkeson, rife with history; the bulb farms of Puyallup ablaze in spring with daffodils and tulips; the authentic Indian salmon bakes on Blake Island—just a short ferry ride across Puget Sound; the harbor tours; a ride on an antique steam engine in Snoqualmie; the glories of Mount Rainier National Park, and tours of the magnificent Victorian homes in Port Townsend. One could travel to a different spot every weekend for a year, and still have sights yet unseen.

Seattle, long considered a kind of "country cousin" in the arts, has come of age with its own symphony, opera company, and repertory company. The Science Center on the grounds of Seattle Center (constructed for the World's Fair in 1962, with an eye to the future) cannot be surpassed anywhere in the country.

In the last few years, Seattle has become a city of "sports nuts"—with the construction of the magnificent domed stadium, "The Kingdome." There are the Mariners (baseball), the Seahawks (football), the Sounders (soccer), and, of course, the Seattle Sonics, the world champion professional basketball team in 1978-1979. Seattleites jog, bicycle—and even roller skate—around Green Lake Park, and there are tennis courts everywhere.

Gourmets will find that Seattle's cuisine ranges from superbly prepared seafood to all variations of oriental food, and a large selection of Greek, French, Mexican, Italian, health foods, and good old meat and potatoes. Prices range from budget to the sky's-the-limit. But the views available to diners are not relative to the price on the menu; some of the most modestly priced restaurants offer a vista of Puget Sound that is unforgettable.

Seattle is a city built on hills, a city where lots are spacious and, like the restaurants, views of the mountains and waters around the city are the rule rather than the exception. If the pioneer fathers who first settled on Alki Point could see what has become of the city they founded, they would be proud and amazed at the changes that have taken place in the last century. Seattle is now, with the heritage of the pioneers, enhanced by the dreams of the Seattleites of the twentieth century.

Downtown Seattle

I have lived in many cities and many states—Michigan, Pennsylvania, Texas, New York, and Oregon. But from the first moment I saw Seattle, on a misty Sunday too many years ago to mention, I knew I had come home at last. To this day, I find myself stopping in a kind of wonderment as I walk along Third Avenue and catch a glimpse of the ferry boats criss-crossing Puget Sound. There is something in the air: good, salty sea air so fresh and invigorating that it makes me say to myself, "I am so *lucky* to be here!" No matter how long you live in Seattle, the sheer joy of the city can catch up with you at unexpected moments.

Downtown is an area of looming skyscrapers that seem almost to spring like mushrooms in the business district, cutting into the skyline to such a height that they must have warning lights for airplanes. They are splendid in their own way, but I prefer the old Seattle, hard by the shores of Elliott Bay, with funny narrow little streets, and places like Ivar Haglund's snack bar where you can buy fish and chips, and toss the leftovers to the insistent gulls. Haglund has many more impressive restaurants, including one atop the Smith Tower.

From Pier 51 to Pier 70, there are a myriad of things to see, from the nameless petrified man in the Olde Curiosity Shop to hundreds of items in import stores. At Pier 59, the Seattle Aquarium lets you come almost nose-to-nose through the glass with such lively water creatures as otters, seals, sting rays, octopi, eels and almost anything that swims, all in carefully reconstructed native habitats. Waterfront Park, one of the city's newer additions, allows an unequaled view of the bay from its two-level decks. There's a place there to fish, a fountain, and rows of trees.

A few blocks above the waterfront are Pioneer and Occidental Squares. Here, one can feel as if he's stepped into a time tunnel—particularly since selected Seattle Police Officers, all tall and mustachioed, wear the uniform that their predecessors did at the turn of the century. They are there to stop crime, but they will also answer questions and happily pose for pictures. You can buy a "take out" sandwich and eat it on the benches in Pioneer Square, while watching the tourists and local habitues pass by, or you can eat at one of the many sidewalk cafes. The proud old brick buildings on the squares have had face lifts, but the essence of the past is still there. There are more shops full of unusual merchandise and some real bargains in the Smith Tower, the Grand Central Building, and the Pioneer Building. On Thursday afternoons in summer, there is live music in Occidental Park. If you are adventurous, join the crowd for the tumultous Fat Tuesday celebration in Occidental Park—and the streets surrounding it—during the Lenten Season. It's rowdy, wild, and unpredictable.

The International District is close by with its Hing Hay and Kobe Parks, tiny but exquisite. Uajimaya's is a genuine Japanese supermarket, jam-packed with exotic food items and oriental wonders. Seattle's Chinatown is the third largest in America, and its restaurants range from ''family style'' one-room spots with incredibly good food, to large and ornate establishments where the food is just as good.

The term ''Skid Road'' was coined in Seattle in early logging days. Yesler Street was once a dirt grade where logs were literally ''skidded'' downhill to the waterfront to be moved out by boat. Today, ''Skid Road'' is the home of men—and women—who have left the mainstream of life. Yesler is part of their territory, and they doze on benches on sunny days in the park next to the King County Courthouse. Yesler is a paved street like any other in Seattle today, and the term ''on the skids'' now applies to the unfortunates who populate Skid Roads in every major city.

Moving north, one can find one of the most innovative uses for a freeway overpass ever devised. Between 6th and 9th Streets, from University to Seneca, The Freeway Park provides an oasis in the very middle of the city. Below, eight lanes of Interstate 5 are continually alive with traffic, but the waterfalls and fountains in the park muffle the sound. Zinnias, marigolds, petunias, rhododendrons, and evergreens have turned the park into a delightful area where brown-baggers can eat lunch at midday, and children can romp in the fountains. The Seattle Park Department provides a free lunch concert for two hours each Tuesday noon during the summer months. At night, colored lights illuminate the fountains.

One of the most popular spots in downtown Seattle for decades has been the creaky old structure that houses the Pike Place Market. It is a jerry-built building with sloping floors, and additions joined to it willy-nilly, and it has a spirit and style all its own. It is currently being rebuilt—but market afficionados have been successful in their fight to ensure that the market retains its funky flavor.

There is probably nothing in the way of foodstuffs that cannot be purchased at the Pike Place Market. Each morning, truck farmers arrive before dawn with produce from the rich soil outside of Seattle. Some have had the same stalls for 40 years. The shopper is transfixed with row upon row of the freshest and best fruits and vegetables in the area. Free samples and haggling over price are all part of the fun. Bargain hunters know that prices late Saturday are the best. There are barrels of fresh clams, shrimp, Dungeness crabs, salmon, mussels—every kind of seafood imaginable. There are meat markets, spice shops, tea and coffee shops, real fresh peanut butter with no preservatives—served up in little white cartons (the kind we used to buy goldfish in). Independent craftsmen offer jewelry, leather goods, candles, stained glass, batik, all of good quality and one-of-a-kind. Strolling musicians add to the atmosphere. DeLaurenti's International Food Market sells bulk pasta, beans and rice, frozen ravioli, manicoti, and fillo leaves. Cheese shops have feta cheese, Jarlsberg, Gouda, Camembert—cheeses called for in the most exotic recipes.

There are no shopping carts, and shopping bags invariably become so weighty with their surfeit of great buys that shoppers swear ''Never again!'' But, of course, they don't really mean it.

With all the bountiful merchandise to choose from, the heart of the market is still its people. Both the sellers and the buyers come to recognize each other. The banter is delightful, and any pretty girl will get a peach or a bunch of grapes from the gallant green grocers simply because she has a nice smile.

Seattle Center has to be considered part of downtown Seattle; it is only a minute-long ride on the Monorail from the center of the city, and its 74 acres were deliberately picked so that the benefits of the buildings built for the 1962 World's Fair would be available to both the inner-city residents and those farther removed. The symbol of that Fair, the Space Needle, dominates Seattle's horizon from every direction, soaring an improbable 500 plus feet into the air on its slender base, standing guard over the Center grounds. Exterior elevators that seem to be suspended in space whisk visitors to the observation deck above in a stomach-churning 43 seconds. From the top of the Space Needle, visitors can see what seems to be the whole world—and certainly all of Seattle and the Puget Sound region. The Space Needle Restaurant revolves, making a complete circle each hour. Diners are treated to a continually changing vista as they eat—yet at a pace so slow they need have no fear of sea-sickness!

The gigantic Center House on the Center grounds has 16 food operations within its sky-lit walls. One can munch and stroll, partaking of all manner of food: pizza, hot dogs, egg rolls, Belgian waffles with whipped cream and strawberries. The elevator (affectionately known as the Bubble-ator because of its shape and clear sides) carries visitors to a level below filled with shops, and, above, to boutiques and the Earl of Sandwich restaurant which features excellent soup, salad, and sandwiches.

Seattle Center houses the Opera House which is known internationally as host to Wagner's momentous *Der Ring des Nibelungen*, four operas sung each year in both German and English. For opera buffs, the 18-hour series is a peak experience. For music lovers of less grandiose tastes, the Opera House also plays host to popular singers and rock bands, and there are many free concerts on the Center grounds. During the Bumbershoot Festival in mid-summer, there are so many free musical and dramatic events on the Center grounds that it's hard to choose which to attend.

The Seattle Repertory Company, with an excellent local company and frequent "big name" guest artists, occupies the Playhouse on the Center grounds from autumn to spring. The Rep players also give free performances each summer in parks all over the city.

The graceful white arches of the Pacific Science Center have become as much a landmark in Seattle and The Center as the Space Needle. To enter the Science Center is to step into a world that titillates the imagination with a recreation of the surging center of a volcano, and a model that duplicates Puget Sound's tidal cycles and currents. In the Starlab Planetarium, the night sky itself is simulated. The Laserium, a throbbing, all-encompassing fusion of color and music, is an integral part of the Science Center, as much a draw for adults as for teenagers.

There is as much to see at Seattle Center as there was during the days of the great fair, all in carefully tended gardens where colored lights play over soaring fountain displays and impromptu concerts abound.

Visitors to Seattle—conventioners, businessmen, or tourists, may choose from a variety of hotels and motels, but the three most unusual are The Olympic Hotel, The Edgewater Inn, and the Washington Plaza, all in the downtown area.

The Olympic was built in 1924, and was considered the grandest hostelry around. Much of Seattle's history has taken place in The Olympic, and visiting presidents have enjoyed its presidential suite for half a century. It is still the largest hotel in Seattle: 800 rooms, five restaurants, lounges, and shops. There is a grand ballroom which has revived the tea dances of an earlier day, and there are sweeping staircases with balustrades, chandeliers, plush carpeting, and valet doors so that one can leave clothes to be pressed—without ever being disturbed. There was talk that The Olympic was to be torn down a few years ago to make way for "progress," but wiser heads prevailed and it has since been nominated a historical Seattle building.

The Washington Plaza is a soaring cylindrical building over 30 stories high, offering awesome views from every window. It is The Olympic of the 1970s and as plush as anyone might want. Trader Vic's restaurant opens just off the lobby. This great, round tower has become a familiar part of Seattle's skyline.

The Edgewater Inn—just as its name says—sits right on the edge of the water, Elliott Bay to be exact. You can fish from your room window on the water side of the inn, or just sit and watch the ships go by.

Downtown Seattle has something for everyone's taste and everyone's pocketbook. Much of the sightseeing is free, and the rest moderately priced. Food isn't free, nor are lodgings, but a little shopping around and a visitor can find something suitable.

Seattle's Waterways

Water, water everywhere in Seattle. The city's eastern boundary is Lake Washington, a huge fresh water lake that extends all along the city's length, and via two floating bridges, connects the communities of Mercer Island and Bellevue. The first and southernmost bridge was considered an engineering miracle when it was built in the 1940s, floating on pontoons. The second, The Evergreen Point Floating Bridge, was able to suspend its toll in June of 1979, more than a decade sooner than predicted because of the mass of vehicles using it.

From the bridges and the shoreline, drivers and residents are treated to the sight of dozens of sailboats, gliding gracefully over the waters of Lake Washington. On stormy days when the wind whips the lake's waters to a frenzy, spray cascades across the bridges, nature tamed but undaunted.

The infinitely dangerous and exhilarating sport of hydroplane racing has one of its main headquarters on Lake Washington where the mighty hydros gather at the Stan Sayres Hydro pits each August during Seafair (*the* festival in a city in love with festivals and parades). Lake Washington's shoreline is inundated with fans who watch the huge boats throw ''rooster-tails'' of spray as they achieve speeds well over a hundred miles an hour, literally soaring on top of the water. Seattle hydro drivers number prominently among the world champions of the sport. For less daring water lovers, there are quiet canoe rides, and public swimming beaches dotted all along Lake Washington.

Seattle's western limits are the salt-water depths of Elliott Bay and Puget Sound; it is here where the great ships come and go, bearing their cargo from every port in the world. Ferries traverse the Sound, carrying sightseers and commuters back and forth to the islands—Blake, Bainbridge, Vashon—where the lifestyle is quieter. The Sound is always alive with activity, and a harbor tour is a must for visitors. Puget Sound, an ideal location for shipping ports, is what made Seattle live and grow, although it is doubtful that the early entrepeneurs could have foreseen the city of Seattle as it is today.

There is no better vista of Seattle than that seen as the mighty—and not-so-mighty—ships approach her western shore. The older buildings cluster close to the water; and the new Seattle, the gigantic monoliths of modern day architecture, rise almost protectively just beyond.

Lake Union lies north of the downtown area. The most optimistic of Seattle's forefathers once predicted that Seattle might one day grow until it extended to Lake Union; today the lake exists almost in the very center of Seattle! It has long been the site of a particularly ''Seattle'' brand of lifestyle—the houseboat. Docks stretch out from the shorelines on all sides of Lake Union, lined with floating homes. Houseboaters are a community unto themselves, a small town right in the middle of a metropolis, and there is a camaraderie and mutual protective society among the water dwellers found nowhere else in the city. Every deck is abloom with flowers, vegetable gardens and even trees, and one has only to roll off his own front porch to enjoy a cooling swim. Most houseboats have some manner of boat tied up alongside—from modest dinghies to 45-foot sail or power boats.

The early houseboats were simple, one-story structures built on logs with whatever materials were available. Today, and somewhat sadly for nostalgia buffs, houseboats are fast becoming the province of the wealthy. The informal houseboats of old are being replaced by multi-storied mansions that sell for up to $250,000.

Still, some of the old-timers remain, and neighborliness prevails, sometimes taking the form of unique ''community'' activity. If logs need to be replaced, a ''stringer'' party is held and the docks are lined with tables sagging with enough food to do credit to a family reunion, while volunteer divers work to replace rotting logs with great blocks of styrofoam. A heavy snowfall is an immediate threat to houseboaters and everyone takes to the roofs to shovel furiously—before the weight of the snow can cause homes to sink.

Green Lake lies several miles north, another oasis for city dwellers. Ducks paddle serenely on the water, and picnickers and kite flyers are everywhere—as well as the aforementioned joggers and roller-skaters. Grandparents and children alike throw in fishing lines and toddlers wade in shallow pools constructed just for them.

Seattle is a boater's paradise, and the community of Ballard in the city's northwest corner is the hub of boating and fishing activities. Ballard is the stronghold of Seattle's huge Scandinavian population, and here commercial fishermen follow the calling of their fathers and grandfathers from the old country. Just south of the Ballard Bridge, at the Salmon Bay Fishermen's Terminal, one can view the largest salmon and halibut fishing fleets in America. Gillnetters, trollers, seiners, tenders, and all manner of commercial fishing ships come in from the sea with their catches, spread their nets along the docks for repairs, and compare notes on how the fish are running.

From the Pacific Ocean through the Sound, both pleasure and commercial craft pass through the Ballard Locks (The Herman Crittenden Locks) and visitors can watch the vessels being raised from six to 26 feet (depending on the tide) in the gigantic locks. The locks cost $2,000,000 to construct and include a fish ladder and an underground viewing window where runs of salmon, steelhead, and trout can be observed at close range.

The Shilshole Bay Marina, the biggest in Seattle, is also in Ballard—row upon row of tall-masted pleasure boats. Even so, Seattleites are so entranced by boating that there is a five to seven year waiting list to gain a berth at Shilshole. The boats bob continually and there is an almost musical "chink-chunk-chink" as their lines and fittings respond to the wind. It is the song of the harbor, omnipresent and exotic in its promise of the voyages that lie ahead. Since most Puget Sound residents consider boat ownership much the way other folks look upon a second car, more marinas are being built in the area all the time.

Space Needle, Seattle Center

Pier 55 and sightseeing boat

State Seal, Seattle Center
(Following pages) Night view across Elliott Bay

Sunset from atop Space Needle

Seattle from Kracke Park

23

Seattle from Kerry Park

Mt. Rainier

25

Magnolia Park

Seattle Center Fountain and Sky Ride

Pioneer Square Park

City Center at night

Duwamish Head Park

Paradise River

Seattle from Seward Park
(Following pages) Seattle and Mt. Rainier from Queen Anne Hill

Sidewalk Cafe near Pioneer Square

Inside Food Circus at Seattle Center

Salmon Bay Fishermen's Terminal

Kingdome and Mt. Rainier

Waterfront Park, Pier 59

A Puget Sound ferry

Space Needle, International Fountain

Moon over Elliott Bay

Pacific Science Center

Puget Sound from Waterfront Park

University of Washington campus

Space Needle from Second Avenue, early morning
(Following pages) Mt. Rainier

Alki Point Lighthouse

51

Marine traffic on Puget Sound

Space Needle from Seattle Center

57

Stairway to Pike Place Market

King Street Train Station

Space Needle and Waterfront

Lake Union from the Space Needle

63

Sunset, Alki Beach

64

Parks

Seattle's Woodland Park Zoo has grown in scope and imagination until it rivals any zoo in the country. Visitors entering at the Fremont Street entrance are treated to the sight of an enchanting formal rose garden. The animals benefit as well: the natural habitats of the over 1,200 animals in the zoo have been faithfully duplicated. The walk-through waterfowl exhibit is a replica of marshlands of New England. A tropical island, the natural habitat of endangered Asian primates, is incredibly real. Under construction is the most natural Gorilla compound to be found in any zoo. A five-acre African Savanna is almost completed. There, lions, giraffes, zebra, springbok, and hippopatomi can cavort as they would in their homeland. There is a reptile house with dozens of species, a Nocturnal House—the only facility of its sort west of the Mississippi—devoted to night creatures of such bizarre types as elephant shrews, sugar gliders, and fruit bats.

The Children's Zoo is full of delightful baby animals, and small visitors are allowed to touch some of the wee creatures.

Volunteer Park, high atop Capital Hill, is one of Seattle's older parks and home for the Seattle Art Museum. It has something for everybody, all nestled in lushly planted grounds. The Museum has a continually changing series of exhibits, from American artists' work to ancient Oriental art objects, Norwegian folk arts and crafts, and calligraphy. It is well worth seeing.

Volunteer Park also houses the city's conservatory, where species grow that would never survive in Seattle's native climate: bananas, rare orchids, Birds of Paradise, and scores of plants more at home on a tropical island. For hearty folks in top condition, there is a brick water tower on the south side of the park where visitors can climb the 106 steps to the 75 foot observation deck and catch a full 360-degree view of Seattle. Volunteer Park has free Sunday afternoon concerts featuring everything from bluegrass to chamber music. Private groups have used park facilities for such functions as bare-footed weddings, 18th century costume picnics, string quartets, and rallies for folks of all persuasions.

Perhaps the most resplendent showcase for floral display in Seattle is in the Arboretum, where bushes and flowers bloom almost year-round. Here, rhododendrons, azaleas, magnolias, heathers, mountain laurel, vine maples, dogwood, and hundreds of other species can be seen from the winding roads that curve through the park. The four-acre Japanese tea garden is designed to place a visitor in Japan itself, with its delicate bridges, quiet ponds, and tea house.

Gasworks Park is built around the stark remains of the now-defunct gasworks on Union Bay, and has a charm all its own. There are innovative crawling and climbing structures which will entrance youngsters for hours.

Gold Rush Park, more of a historical museum than a sylvan park, opened recently in Pioneer Square. Exhibits recall the glorious day when the vessel *Excelsior* landed in Seattle on July 17, 1897 with more than a ton of Alaskan gold aboard. Visitors can see, for free, photomurals of Old Seattle and actual reconstructed mining equipment. A 117-seat theater shows slides on the Gold Rush, and the University of Washington's School of Drama offers a free play on weekends titled ''Gold Fever.''

Marymoor Park, in the King County suburb of Redmond, is the largest park in the county. The historic Clise Mansion and its windmill, both built in 1904, remain today as the hub of the park. There are football and soccer fields, tennis courts, and the only bike velodrome in the State of Washington.

Seattle, true to form, is now looking forward to a park of mammoth proportions, soon to be built on the extensive grounds of the phased-out Sand Point Naval Air Station on Lake Washington.

Out-Of-Town Trips

Starting from the center of Seattle, there are almost as many things to do and places to see as one could ever imagine, all within two to four hours travel time.

Deep-sea fishermen—or would-be fishermen—can drive to Westport, "The Salmon Fishing Capital of the World" where some 350 charter fishing boats await. Salmon is the optimum catch, but there are also tuna and bottom fish to be found. In season, there is good fishing in the scores of lakes around Seattle, and in Puget Sound.

City Light's Skagit Tours offer a bird's eye view of Seattle's tremendous hydroelectric project and feature a trip on an incline railway, a boat ride on Diablo Lake—a lake of such inpenetrable blue that it dazzles the eye—a tour of the Ross Dam Powerhouse and a close look at the awesome North Cascade range.

A real ocean voyage—albeit a short one—on the Princess Marguerite takes travelers to Victoria B.C. in four hours. There, the dowager of all grand hotels, The Empress, offers a genuine high English tea, and exquisite formal gardens. There are museums and shops to see, and transportation is by horse-drawn wagons.

Blake Island, a tiny outcropping of land in Puget Sound, can be reached in an hour or so aboard a tour boat, and is renowned for its Tillicum Village Salmon bakes—cooked just as the Indians have done for centuries. There are freshly dug steamed clams, salmon baked in a deep pit, hot bread, and fresh blackberry pie. The Indian longhouse is full of Indian antiques and dancers perform the ancient dances.

White-river rafting is available, on one-day or longer trips, on rushing rivers east of Seattle. For the brave, the rafts will plow through the churning waters and over falls; for the scenery buffs, there are less ambitious river routes. Some deluxe day-tours include champagne and steak.

Snoqualamie Falls offers a breathtaking view of the Falls from vantage points where the spray of the deluge fills the air—or from the more comfortable dining room of the Snoqualmie Falls Lodge, famous for its country breakfasts—oatmeal, hotcakes, ham, bacon, eggs, and homemade biscuits and honey. It's all within an hour of Seattle.

Mount Rainier is 14,410 feet above sea level, and one of the biggest, though not the highest mountain in the contiguous 48 states. Rainier is a two-hour drive from Seattle and is criss-crossed with trails for hikers. There are lodges with restaurants and snack bars, and overnight accommodations. Rainier is also a formidable challenge for trained mountain climbers—both summer and winter—but the climb is not for the neophyte.

Take a 55-minute cruise across the Sound to Bremerton, famed for its Navy Yard. The *USS Missouri*, the battleship on which the Japanese surrendered in 1945, is permanently docked in Bremerton and open to visitors. The trip over and back affords some of the best scenery in the state as the ferry winds its way through Elliott Bay, Rich Passage, and Sinclair Inlet. On a clear day, both Mount Rainier and Mount Baker can be seen in all their glory.

Skiers flock to Snoqualmie, Stevens, and White Pass from November through March in a good snow year—all easy one day trips.

Between spring and fall, the mountain passes take on a different quality. The snow melts from all but the highest peaks and the vegetation changes—save for the towering evergreen trees on all sides—from the pastels of May to the fiery red and gold leaves of October. A picnic atop a mountain meadow in summer is worth the climb, and there are cool lakes to swim and fish in.

Seattle wasn't the only port city on the Sound in the 1800s. Many of the others have been preserved, and they make for fascinating visits. At one time, Port Townsend, on the very northeast tip of the Olympic Peninsula, was heralded as the future metropolis of Puget Sound. In its boom days of the 1880s, it had six banks, three street railroads, and a natural harbor second only to New York City. But the crash of 1890 destroyed all the dreams of Port Townsend, and today it is a sleepy little town, a Victorian spinster left with her memories. Yet the mansions remain, symbols of another time. They stand proudly, freshly painted, replete with turrets, gingerbread, and widows' walks. Some are said to be haunted—and well they may be—by the women who waited for their men to come home from the sea.

Port Gamble, a short ferry ride from the northern boundaries of Seattle, was once the site of a booming lumber town, located ideally on Hood Canal as it led into the Strait of Juan de Fuca. The company buildings and the neat little workers' houses are still there, along with the company store. Many of the first industries of old Seattle have given way to fortune and time, but others have taken their place.

Seattle's founding fathers, who foresaw greatness because of the harbor, had never heard—or even imagined—such a thing as an airplane, and yet it was an outgrowth of that invention that was to become the solid foundation of Seattle's

68

economy: the Boeing Company. In 1978, Boeing was awarded a magnificent $12 billion in orders to supply their mighty jets to airlines all over the world. Visitors can watch the assembly of a 747 from a viewing platform inside the world's largest building—part of Boeing's Everett complex, 30 miles north of Seattle. The Boeing tours are free and include a half-hour movie describing the company's operations.

After the tour, it is but a 15 minute trip west into the quaint seaside town of Mukilteo. There are shops there, and restaurants featuring superb seafood and a view of the Sound and shipping lanes.

In Kirkland, a hop-skip-and jump from Seattle across the Evergreen Point Floating Bridge, three historic ships are berthed at the Moss Bay Marina: the *Arthur Foss*, a vintage steam tug, the *Wawona*, last of the Northwest's tall ships, and the steam-powered lightship, *Relief*. The *Arthur Foss*, a veteran of the Gold Rush, was, incredibly, still in service in World War II and the last vessel out of Wake Island. The *Wawona* has been lovingly restored by sailing ship buffs who could not bear to see her lost to time and decay.

One of Seattle's newest industries is the Chateau Ste. Michelle Winery near Woodenville, a few miles north of Kirkland. Heralded by wine experts, the winery is styled after a French country estate, and visitors can observe the wine-making process from the time the grapes arrive from the vineyards of Eastern Washington, through fermentation, racking and filtration, barrel aging, bottling, and bottle aging. There is also the fun of the final stage—tasting. The tour is free.

Ambience

If there is one word to describe the essence of Seattle, it is enthusiasm. There is an intensity among Seattleites, almost a naiveté in its citizens' enjoyment. No one is blasé, Seattle, in the vast spectrum of time, simply hasn't been around long enough to become so worldly that nothing is exciting. In Seattle, everything is exciting.

In the age-old science of astrology, Seattle's beginnings make her a Scorpio city. Indeed, the whole State of Washington is a Scorpio state—both founding dates corresponding with a Scorpio birthdate. And Scorpio is the most intense sign in the Zodiac. Perhaps it is myth; perhaps it is true, but the ambience in Seattle is one of delight, of wonder, and of continual appreciation of what Seattle has to offer.

When the Super Sonics won the 1978-79 World Championship, more than half the city turned out to honor them in such a tumultous parade that it seemed the buildings themselves would rock off their foundations. Police and citizens alike cheered and waved. It is the same with Seafair Parades, with the numberless neighborhood fairs, with Fat Tuesday. If something is happening, Seattleites jump right in and participate. They are the city . . .and the city is them.

People who meet on the street—strangers—tend to smile; there is not the averting of eyes seen in Eastern cities. If you move to Seattle, it doesn't take years to become part of the gang. You live here, so you belong, and where you lived last month doesn't matter. In a poll taken by a national magazine in 1978, Seattle was chosen as the number one city that readers would like to live in—if they could. And so, in spite of the tongue-in-cheek ''Lesser Seattle'' campaigns, the population is bound to grow, and there will be more Seattleites ''singing in the rain.''

There is a great ''caring'' for people in Seattle. This is reflected in programs initiated in city government. There is a ''Magic Carpet''—free bus service—in downtown areas, and oldsters ride all buses at lowered prices.

Seattle's Fire Department began the ''Medic I'' paramedic program which has served as a model for emergency medical care for fire departments all over America.

70

That same department has initiated an arson control program that has made Seattle the most arson-free city in the country. Of all major cities in the United States, Seattle is the only one where loss from arson is going down . . .instead of up.

Seattle had the first Crisis Clinic in the country—a phone line to people in deep emotional distress. This concept has spread to hundreds of other cities, but it was Seattle's Crisis Clinic that led the way, and it was featured in the Sidney Poitier—Ann Bancroft movie, "The Slender Thread."

Even the down-and-outers along Skid Road are looked after. When a number of vagrants were being robbed of what little they had while they slept in alley-ways, Seattle policemen disguised themselves as raggedy tramps and served as decoys. Those who preyed on the helpless were mightily surprised to find a big, strong cop responding to someone searching his pockets, and the robbing of vagrants diminished by a marked degree.

Seattle isn't perfect; no city is, but it offers much of the best living around—natural beauty, prudent city planning, environmental control, a variety of experiences, and a population both friendly and concerned for its fellow man. And, while the air is still clean, the waters still pure, the mountains still standing proud, and the rain still falling, Seattle intends to remain the city most sought after as home.

Beautiful America Publishing Company

The nation's foremost publisher of quality color photography

Current Books

Alaska, Arizona, British Columbia, California, California Vol. II, California Coast, California Desert, California Missions, Colorado, Florida, Georgia, Hawaii, Los Angeles, Idaho, Illinois Maryland, Michigan, Michigan Vol. II, Minnesota, Montana, Montana Vol. II, Mt. Hood (Oregon), New York, New Mexico, Northern California, Northern California Vol. II, North Idaho, Oregon, Oregon Vol. II, Oregon Coast, Oregon Mountains, Portland, Pennsylvania, San Diego, San Francisco, Texas, Utah, Virginia, Washington, Washington Vol. II, Washington D.C., Wisconsin, Yosemite National Park

Forthcoming Books

California Mountains, Indiana, Kentucky, Las Vegas, Massachusetts, Mississippi, Missouri, Nevada, New Jersey, North Carolina, Oklahoma, Ozarks, Rocky Mountains, San Juan Islands, Seattle, South Carolina, Tennessee, Vermont, Wyoming

Large Format, Hardbound Books

Beautiful America, Beauty of California, Glory of Nature's Form, Lewis & Clark Country, Western Impressions